Con

Cover photo: Detail of "The Adoration of the Shepherds," by Giorgione; National Gallery of Art, Washington; Samuel H. Kress Collection.

Introduction

The trees had been stripped bare by the winter wind. Frost had turned the rolling fields of eastern Kentucky bluegrass to a lifeless brown. The steel-gray sky gave ominous warning of the winter to come. Advent was heavy upon us when I made my first pilgrimage to the Abbey of Gethsemani. During Advent, nearly three decades earlier, Thomas Merton entered that same monastery, not simply to visit, but to stay. Merton said he could not think of a better time than Advent to begin life as a monk.

You begin a new life, you enter into a new world at the beginning of a new liturgical year. And everything that the Church gives you to sing, every prayer that you say . . . is a cry of ardent desire for grace, for help, for the coming of the Messiah, the Redeemer.[1]

As the cold stones of the old abbey church rang with Gregorian chant, Merton felt a clean, profound desire, drawing him within, until his soul became a Bethlehem where the Son of God could be born.

Advent is more than a pleasant recycling of familiar traditions, more than liturgical marketing to pack the house on Christmas Eve, more than ecclesiastical competition with worship at the shopping mall. Advent is a bold invitation to begin a new life, to enter into a radically new world. When the secular calendar moves into a time of endings, the calendar of faith turns to its beginning. While people in the Northern Hemisphere move toward wintery death, the followers of Jesus, like residents of the Southern Hemisphere, feel the surging promise of new life. Advent pilgrims do not merely celebrate Jesus' birth in the past; we invite God to create a new life within us that we never conceive on our own. This world becomes the arena of God's salvation; each soul becomes a Bethlehem where the Son of God may once again be born.

The Old Testament lessons this year draw us into the prophetic imagination of Isaiah, who saw the word of the Lord as a hope-filled alternative for people on the edge of destruction. The Gospel lessons from Matthew offer a shocking contrast to the lyrical words of Luke, which are the primary source for most of our Christmas traditions. Matthew writes a rugged, masculine story, centered in the experiences of Joseph rather than Mary. Jesus is born into a violent world of oppressive powers, a world where Herod reigns and only a few "wise men" claim Jesus as king. The Epistle lessons celebrate God's saving action in Christ and challenge us to reorder our existence around the promised coming of our Lord.

Heard together, these lessons entice us with the long-hoped-for vision of God's healing alternative for this creation and call us to prepare for the coming of the Son of God by making our lives a present expression of the future fulfillment of God's salvation.

Isaiah announced God's word to the covenant people in Babylon and Jerusalem. Matthew's Gospel was written for a second generation Christian community in which people who believed in Jesus were defining their identity in a hostile world. Paul wrote to fellow Christians who were forming their community around their experience of the risen Lord. In a similar sense, this study is designed to be used in the church, among baptized believers, faithful disciples, or spiritual seekers who are engaged in the life of a Christian community. It is a word spoken to a church that struggles to keep its vision clear in an often confusing and turbulent world.

Biblical scholar Walter Brueggemann sounded like an Old Testament prophet when he described the church as being so acclimated to "the American ethos of consumerism that it has little power to believe or to act."[2] We have become so much a part of the commonly assumed values and convictions of the world around us that we have lost the transforming power of a prophetic vision. Brueggemann declared that the task of prophetic ministry is to "nurture, nourish, and evoke" an alternative vision of reality to the vision that is assumed by the dominant culture around us.[3] The Scripture lessons for Advent are intended to awaken within the church a fresh vision of God's intention for our world and to empower us to see God's new creation becoming a reality through us.

Remembering my first Advent journey to Gethsemani and preparing for this Advent journey together, I begin with a deep conviction that Merton got it right. There could hardly be a better time to begin a new life, to enter a new world, than at the beginning of a new liturgical year. There could hardly be a better time to imagine a prophetic alternative to the dominant culture around us than Advent. There could hardly be a better time to declare a new vision of God's saving alternative for this world and for our lives than during these weeks as we pray

Come, thou long-expected Jesus,
born to set thy people free;
from our fears and sins release us,
let us find our rest in thee.
Israel's hope and consolation,
hope of all the earth thou art;
dear desire of every nation,
joy of every longing heart.[4]

Charles Wesley

---

[1] From *The Seven Storey Mountain,* by Thomas Merton (Harcourt Brace Jovanovich, Inc., 1948); page 379.

[2] From *The Prophetic Imagination,* by Walter Brueggemann (Fortress Press, 1978); page 11.

[3] From *The Prophetic Imagination;* page 13.

[4] During a visit to Bristol, England, I purchased a facsimile of the first edition of Charles Wesley's *Hymns for the Nativity of our Lord,* published in 1745. While at least one of his Christmas hymns has become a universal favorite ("Hark! The Herald Angels Sing"), some of his lesser known texts have enriched my spiritual journey as well. I have included some of those texts in this study because of their spiritual insight.

God's Alternative Reality

Scriptures for Advent:
The First Sunday
Isaiah 2:1-5
Matthew 24:36-44
Romans 13:11-14

Ken Burns, the movie producer who brought the Civil War and the history of baseball to public television, has done it again. This time he followed the Lewis and Clark expedition into the unknown frontier of the Great Northwest in search of a passage to the Pacific Ocean. I was "channel surfing" when I came upon the program, but it hooked my attention immediately. By the time Burns reached the headwaters of the Missouri River, I felt—along with the historians on the screen—a huge lump in my throat as I sensed the impact of that moment. They expected to find a direct water route to the Pacific Ocean. They expected to put their canoes into the river at the Continental Divide and be carried down to the shore. But when they looked over the crest of the hills, they saw the Rocky Mountains. The sight must have taken their breath away. Their discovery was a momentous alternative reality to everything they expected or imagined.

If we allow ourselves to be drawn into the prophetic vision of the lessons for the first Sunday in Advent, we may begin to feel that we are standing on the edge of something utterly new—something long-awaited, long-anticipated, long-promised, but something totally beyond our human capacity to fulfill. Our eyes will be opened to a shocking alternative to the day-to-day realities we have come to expect. The promises of Advent open our souls to a Spirit-energized vision of God's healing alternative for the world.

In the Old Testament lesson, Isaiah sees "the mountain of the LORD's house . . . as the highest of the mountains" (2:1). From that height, we catch a glimpse of God's intention for a world at peace. It is the divine alternative to the conflict, destruction, and violence of both the world into which the prophecy was spoken and the world in which we live. The Gospel lesson gives us a momentary glimpse of the apocalyptic fulfillment of the coming of the Son of Man as we hear Jesus challenge his followers to keep awake for the coming of the day of the Lord. The epistle underscores the urgency of the time and calls us to shape our lives in the present around the promised reality of God's salvation, which will be fulfilled in the future. As this living word penetrates our slumbering spirits, we are awakened to a vision of life in a new world. There is every possibility that what we see will take our breath away. It offers a momentous alternative reality to everything we have come to expect in this world.

A national journal, which identified him as "a pioneering pioneer" among pastors and teachers of world religions, reported Huston Smith's concern for what he called a "stifling accommodation to worldly styles of thought" within the mainline churches in America today. He concluded with this haunting question: "If churches do not present people with a momentous alternative reality to the one that bombards them every day, why should people complicate their already harried and fragmented lives with another institution?"[1]

Why, indeed, should people who live fragmented and harried lives turn to the church? Why should people interrupt the excitement of the "holiday" season to experience a "holy day" in worship? Do we offer a life-transforming, monumental alternative reality for the limited realities of the world in which we live?

THE SEASON OF IMAGINATION
Isaiah 2:1-5

The sights, songs, sounds, and stories of Advent tingle with anticipation and ignite our imagination. Children imagine the patter of reindeer hoofs or the flutter of angel wings. They visualize a Grinch who set out to steal Christmas, only to discover that he could not stop it if he tried. Adults imagine the joy of Ebenezer Scrooge as he awoke from his ghost-filled night or George Bailey's tear-jerking discovery that "It's a Wonderful Life" after all. On Christmas Eve, we imagine ourselves among the shepherds who first heard the angel choirs or see ourselves in the company of the wise men who knelt before the child with their gifts.

As I write these words, I can look out my study window to watch a children's Christmas party going on across the street. Imagination-impaired adults know that the little brown pony with the red Santa blanket on his back is only circling the block, but I suspect—no, I am quite sure—that the squealing preschooler who is taking the ride is fully capable of imagining that he is headed to the North Pole. More than any other time of year, this season has the power to awaken the gift of imagination within us.

Imagination is not just for Christmas, and it is not just for kids. Albert Einstein declared that "imagination is more important than knowledge." Peter M. Senge, representing the world of secular organizational leadership and management, writes that the ability to grasp a "shared picture of the future we seek to create" is essential to every successful organization.[2] More than one political candidate has fallen short of success because he or she just did not get "the vision thing." In many ways, the world around us confirms the conclusion of Scripture that without vision, without the gift of imagination, people perish (Proverbs 29:18, King James Version).

Spirit-energized imagination was central to the calling of the Old Testament prophets. They practiced what Walter Brueggemann called "futuring fantasy," a wonderful phrase that sounds a little like something that might come from the "Imagineers" at Disney World. Brueggemann said the primary vocation of the biblical prophets was "to keep alive the ministry of imagination, to keep on conjuring and proposing alternative futures."[3]

The text before us is "the word that Isaiah son of Amoz saw concerning Judah and Jerusalem." The Spirit of God opened Isaiah's imagination to see God's alternative reality in, through, and beyond the distressing realities of his time. God's redeeming work for Jerusalem began with a Spirit-energized imagination, a visualized announcement of the future that God intended to create.

Isaiah's vision is recorded as a poem. This is not the cold, flat, factual prose of a news reporter but the evocative language of a poet. The Greek word *poetes* means "maker." The task of a poet is not necessarily to explain things but to make something happen in the mind, heart, and soul of the reader. Contrary to public opinion, the biblical prophets were not crystal ball-gazing fortune tellers. They were visionary poets whose words were intended to make something happen in the imagination of the reader. Their inspired visions were meant to evoke feelings, images, and alternative ways of seeing reality that would reform the life of the community of faith around God's new alternative for their future. The prophetic texts have the power to release within each of us the "futuring fantasy" of God's vision for this world.

How do the sights, songs, sounds, and stories of this season touch your imagination?

When have you experienced imagination as a gift of the Spirit?

What "futuring fantasy" has God given to you?

Jerusalem was a vulnerable city in a tiny nation that constantly faced the very real possibility of destruction by the aggressive nations that surrounded it. In Isaiah's time, the ever-looming adversary was Assyria, the invincible military superpower of the day. The center of the city, indeed the center of life for the covenant people, was Zion, "the mountain of the LORD's house." The "center of the center" was the Temple itself, the locus of God's presence on earth.

In Chapter 1, Isaiah sees all too clearly the political arrogance, crass immorality, and self-serving religion that would lead—as it always does—to destruction. He describes the expected reality of life in a tough, violent, power-hungry, and sinful world. In Chapter 2, however, the prophet sees God's momentous alternative. It is the soul-stirring vision of Zion as the highest of all mountains. People from all nations (not just the Hebrews) stream into it to learn God's way and to walk in God's paths. All of life is reoriented around the will and purpose of God.

As a kid growing up in a small town in Pennsylvania, I developed an enduring fantasy of spending Christmas in New York, the city that has identified itself as "The Capital of the World." That attitude was captured in a famous painting of *A New Yorker's View of the World*. Manhattan is in bold clarity, with the Hudson River as the edge of the globe. The rest of the continent is little more than a sliver of unknown and unimportant geography beyond it.

A New Yorker's View of the World conveys the feeling of this text with its vision of Jerusalem as the divine center of the world's existence. A more appropriate comparison might be the Washington National Cathedral. It sits on Mount Saint Albans, the highest point within the District of Columbia. Flying in or out of National Airport, you can see it on the hill, towering above all the buildings and monuments that represent the power, prestige, and strength of the nation. At the heart of the cathedral, above the high altar, is the massive carving of *Christ in Majesty,* seated on a throne, holding the orb of authority in one hand and offering the sign of peace with the other. Dedicated as "a place of prayer for all nations," the cathedral draws people from around the world to worship the God who reigns over all nations, all cultures, all time, and all history. In its ministries of compassion, justice, and peace, the cathedral teaches people of faith how to walk in the paths of the Lord and how to shape their lives in the present around God's vision of the future.

Isaiah sees what no one else can see: the Temple as the spiritual center of reality that reorients the life of the world around the redemptive purpose and redeeming power of God. It is a vision of God's justice, healing, and salvation fulfilled in this very real world. The result is a world at peace. The Lord himself becomes the arbitrator between nations. Swords are turned into plowshares and spears into pruning hooks. Nation no longer lifts up sword against nation, neither do they learn war anymore.

Isaiah's vision was a radical alternative to the cultural assumptions of the people around him. They simply could not imagine a world at peace. I am sure most reasonable, practical folks said, "Isaiah, you've got to be realistic!" They assumed that the only reality was the reality of the world of violence. They were like the military leader who, when the Berlin wall fell, said that we were ready for everything except peace.

Isaiah saw an alternative reality, no less real, though not nearly as obvious. It was the eternal reality of God's redemptive purpose at work within the temporary realities of conflict and evil. He envisioned God's salvation as a momentous alternative to the prevailing assumptions of the culture around him.

Jane Addams was the founder of one of the earliest models of inner city ministry in the nation. Looking at the harsh realities of poverty, pain, injustice, and violence in Chicago, she said that "much of the insensibility and hardness of the world is due to the lack of imagination."[4]

Isaiah's vision forces us to confess that the church in our time suffers from a lack of imagination when it comes to the biblical vision of non-violence and peace. We have become far too comfortable with the assumed realities of a culture of violence. We accept too easily the assumptions of a world that is oriented around coercion and force. If we allow this text to inspire a prophetic vision of peace within us, we are forced to face some very difficult questions.

How much of the conflict and tension of the world in which we live is a result of a lack of Spirit-energized imagination of creative non-violence on the part of the people of God?

How have we accommodated God's alternative reality of peace to the violent realities of a sinful world?

When will we dare proclaim that the eternal reality beneath the noisy, conflicted realities of our time is the message of peace on earth and goodwill to all?

A PEEK AT THE LAST PAGE
Matthew 24:36-44

I confessed in one of my books that when it comes to novels, I am a "compulsive last-page reader." It is hard for me to resist the temptation of taking a peek at the last page to see how the whole thing comes out. I take consolation in knowing that John Steinbeck wrote *The Grapes of Wrath* from the perspective of the final page. He recorded in his journal that he kept his attention "fixed on the last scene, huge and symbolic, toward which the whole story moves."[5]

More recently, I read of the work of Frank Kermode, who did an intensive study of modern forms of apocalyptic literature and came to the conclusion that there is almost a human necessity for what he calls "the sense of an ending."[6] There is within each of us an innate sense that human life and history are going somewhere, that this human drama is headed toward a grand finale, that there will ultimately be some gathering together of all the scattered strands of human history into a coherent and meaningful conclusion.

The writer of the Gospel of Matthew places Jesus' words about the final page of human history in the context of his prediction of the destruction of the Temple (Matthew 24:1-2). That destruction came in A.D. 70, around the time this Gospel was being written. Confronted with the reality of violence and destruction, the eschatological vision of the New Testament is huge and symbolic. It is the final scene toward which the whole of human history moves. We read this "end times" vision on the first Sunday of Advent to declare that the one who came at Bethlehem is the one who will come at the end of time. The one whose story begins in a manger is the one whose story will end on a throne. The celebration of the coming of the Son of God in the past is set within the framework of his final coming in the future.

One of the most famous Christmas Eve services in the world is "A Festival of Lessons and Carols" at King's College, Cambridge, England. It has been broadcast by the BBC every year since 1928. Millions of listeners wait in silence each year for the haunting sound of a young boy's voice that opens the service with the first verse of "Once in Royal David's City." Verse by verse the carol builds in power until the chapel reverberates with the choir and organ declaring its closing affirmations.

And our eyes at last shall see
    him,
    Through his own redeeming
    love;
For that child so dear and
    gentle
Is our Lord in heav'n above;
And he leads his children on
To the place where he is gone.

Not in that poor lowly stable,
With the oxen standing by,
We shall see him; but in
    heaven,
Set at God's right hand on
    high;
When like stars his children
    crowned
All in white shall wait around.[7]

We would do well to allow the lectionary to lead us here. The "mainline" churches have been far too willing to abandon eschatology to those who ardently believe and passionately proclaim some of the most bizarre interpretations of apocalyptic literature in the history of the faith. We could hardly find a better time to lift up the central affirmations of our belief in the final coming of Christ than during Advent.

Several affirmations form the center of biblical faith in the final coming of Christ.

1) The day of the Lord will come (Matthew 24:30). Human history is not a constantly repeating cycle. It is moving toward a day when God's redemptive purpose will be accomplished. In that day God's healing alternative for the world will be fulfilled and Jesus Christ will be Lord of all.

2) The end will be both cosmic and personal. It includes the salvation of human beings and the redemption of the whole created order. In the same paragraph, Matthew records Jesus' description of changes in the planets and of his people being gathered "from the four winds" (Matthew 24:29-31).

3) No one (and that means *no one*) knows or can predict the time. I never cease to be amazed at people who insist on taking the Bible literally but who refuse to take Jesus seriously when he tells us not to try to figure out the calendar date of his final coming (Matthew 24:36). Christian history is littered with the sad remains of the folks who thought they had calculated the date and failed.

4) The task of discipleship is not to predict when or how the end will come but to live as obedient servants, doing the work the Master would be doing if he were here. Being ready for the final coming of Christ means living in the present in ways that are consistent with what we believe about the future (Matthew 24:45-51).

To reinforce his point, Jesus drew a direct comparison to the days of Noah. The folks around Noah lived on the assumption that the way things are is the way things will always be. They were caught up in the ordinary realities of life as they had always experienced it: eating, drinking, marrying, and giving in marriage. "They knew nothing," Jesus said. They could not imagine an alternative to the reality they had known. Noah stood out in the crowd because he acted on the call and promise of God. When no one expected rain, Noah built an ark. Jesus said that's just the way it will be. Some will be taken; some will be left. Some people are awake to see the unexpected coming of the Son of Man, while others are blind to the whole thing. Some will be faithful servants, alert to the coming of their Lord, while others are asleep at the switch.

I saw a bumper sticker that declared: "Jesus is coming soon. Look busy!" Our task is not just to look busy but to look like the present expression of God's alternative reality, which will be fulfilled at the end of time. Charles Wesley prayed for the return of our Lord in this carol:

All glory to God in the sky,
    And peace upon earth be restored!
O Jesus, exalted on high,
    Appear, our omnipotent Lord:
Who meanly in Bethlehem born,

Didst stoop to redeem a lost race,
Once more to thy creature return,
    And reign in thy kingdom of grace.
. . . .

Come then to thy servants again,
    Who long thy appearing to know,
Thy quiet and peaceable reign
    In mercy establish below:
All sorrow before thee shall fly,
    And anger and hatred be o'er,
And envy and malice shall die,
    And discord afflict us no more.

No horrid alarm of war,
    Shall break our eternal repose,
No sound of the trumpet is there,
    Where Jesus's spirit o'erflows:
Appeased by the charms of thy grace,
    We all shall in amity join,
And kindly each other embrace,
    And love with a passion like thine.[8]

What has been your understanding of the final coming of Christ?

How does this word from Jesus help you see the fulfillment of God's purpose in history?

What will it mean for you to live as a faithful disciple of Jesus until he comes again?

WAKE UP TO THE FUTURE!
Romans 13:11-14

The fifty-year-old mantel clock in our dining room was a Christmas gift from my father-in-law. It keeps near-perfect time, but not today. The chimes that announce the quarter hours and hours are out of sync with the face of the clock. This morning, for instance, the digital clock in the bedroom said it was 3:00 A.M. when I counted the chimes ringing twelve times. If we do not wind the clock today, we may never be sure of the correct time!

The first Christians had a specific way of telling the time. They measured all time in relation to the final time when God's purpose would be fulfilled and Christ would come again. The clock of human experience was adjusted toward the huge, symbolic finale toward which all history moved. The first-generation Christians clearly expected Jesus to return in their lifetime. But as that generation passed away, second-generation Christians were forced to readjust their spiritual clocks. They still looked forward to the final day, but they lived every day with a vigorous sense of divine urgency. The vision of God's salvation in the future became the formative reality in the present life of every follower of Christ.

Rabbi and scholar Abraham Heschel once described the passion of the prophets as "the passion of this God who knows what time it is."[9] That same passion flows through Paul's challenge to the Romans to wake from sleep, to put away the works of darkness, and to put on the armor of light. It is the continuing reminder of Jesus' command: "Keep awake therefore, for you do not know on what day your Lord is coming" (Matthew 24:42). The call of the apostle is to live every moment with the urgency of the "last days." It's the only time we've got!

The calling for biblical prophets in every age is to cut through the spiritual numbness, to penetrate the slumbering imagination of God's people, and to awaken within the community of faith a fresh vision of the momentous alternative reality of God's future. We are called to set the clock of our souls in sync with the ultimate fulfillment of God's salvation. Our task is to keep awake for the fulfillment of that vision within and through us.

If we are honest, we know the spiritual numbness. Because of the wear and tear of an often insensitive world, because of the pace and stress of our hyperactive lives, because of the very real pain and suffering that seem to come from nowhere and knock us to the ground, it is easy to become convinced that there are no new possibilities for our lives and our world. We can become so conditioned to the realities of the present that we lose our vision for the future. We become so conditioned by what is that we no longer see what could be. The task of the prophetic word in our experience is to awaken us to the awesome alternative reality of God's invasion of our lives, bringing new possibilities for our future.

When our daughters were young, we had two rules about Christmas morning. First, no one could get up before they could see the sun. Having come through the candle-light service marathon of Christmas Eve, we all needed a few hours of sleep. Second, no one went to the Christmas tree until everyone was awake. It became a Christmas tradition for our daughters to sneak into our bedroom at the first light of dawn, climb into our bed, and tug on our arms as they called out, "Wake Up! It's Christmas!" As they grew older, there were even times when the roles were reversed. Ours, at least, was a kinder, gentler awakening than the one my brother's father-in-law used to give by blowing his bugle.

The apostle Paul shouts that kind of wake up call to the Christians in Rome:

As I think you have realized, the present time is of the highest importance—it is time to wake up to reality. . . The night is nearly over; the day has almost dawned (Romans 13:11, *The New Testament in Modern English*).

To live within the promise of the final coming of our Lord is to know that the present moment is of highest importance. Every moment of life is an opportunity to wake up to the alternative reality of God's salvation that was visualized by the prophets, announced by Jesus, and will be fulfilled at the end of time.

The words of a hymn by F. Bland Tucker offer the call to each of us.

Awake, O sleeper, rise from death,
and Christ shall give you light;
so learn his love, its length and breadth,
its fullness, depth, and height.

For us Christ lived, for us he died,
and conquered in the strife.
Awake, arise, go forth in faith,
and Christ shall give you life.[10]

How does believing in the coming of Christ in the future impact your sense of faithful living in the present?

What will it mean for you to wake up to the urgency of this moment in your life?

What practical changes do you need to make to "lay aside the works of darkness and put on the armor of light"?

---

[1] From "Are Churches Filling the Void?" by Martin E. Marty, in *Context*, October 15, 1995; page 5.

[2] From *The Fifth Discipline*, by Peter M. Senge (Doubleday/Currency, 1990); page 9.

[3] From *The Prophetic Imagination;* page 45.

[4] From *The New York Public Library Book of 20th Century American Quotations*, edited by Stephen Donadio, et al. (The Stonesong Press, Inc., 1992); page 259.

[5] From *God Isn't Finished With Us Yet*, by James Harnish (The Upper Room, 1991); page 100.

[6] From *Reversed Thunder*, by Eugene H. Peterson (Harper Collins, 1988); page 195.

[7] From *The Hymnal of the Protestant Episcopal Church in the United States of America* (The Church Pension Fund, 1940); #236.

[8] From *Christian Year and Occasional Hymns* (The Charles Wesley Society, 1991); pages 45-46.

[9] From *The Prophetic Imagination;* page 53.

[10] Words: Augsburg Fortress; 426 S. Fifth Street, Minneapolis, MN 56440. Used by permission.

A Little Child Shall Lead Them

Scriptures for Advent:
The Second Sunday
Isaiah 11:1-10
Matthew 3:1-12
Romans 15:4-13

We hear it everywhere we go this time of year: "Christmas is for children." In one sense, of course, the folks who share that sentiment are absolutely correct. You would have to be an unrepentant Scrooge not to feel it.

Catch the reflection of a candle flame in the eye of a child who lights an Advent wreath. Chuckle at a shepherd who stumbles into the chancel with his tennis shoes in full view beneath his father's bathrobe. Smile at little girls with tinsel in their hair and cardboard wings attached to their shoulders, awaiting their cue to sing the angels' song.

Christmas is for children. But that "Disney-like" sentiment is light years removed from Isaiah's promise of a Child-King who would bring real changes to the real world in which he would reign. The birth of this Child would create a momentous alternative to the present realities around which people built their lives.

As every new parent has discovered, when you let a child invade your life, everything begins to change. Nothing will ever be the same again. It's the difference between "B.C." (*Before Children*) and "A.D." (*After Delivery*). Picture Christmas in the home of a sophisticated, professional couple. Their elegant china nativity figurines are arranged with care on their glass-topped coffee table. That was *"Christmas, B.C."* In *"Christmas, A.D.,"* the china figurines have been replaced with plastic ones. The pungent scent of potpourri competes with the distinct aroma of diapers and baby powder. The cappuccino maker gathers dust while the washing machine runs full time. Their lives will never be the same again.

Playwright Stephen Vincent Benet expressed the change the Christmas Child brings in the words of the innkeeper's wife. Looking back on that night when they had no room for a woman in labor, she says:

God pity us indeed, for we are human,
And do not always see
The vision when it comes, the shining change,
Or, if we see it, do not follow it,
Because it is too hard, too strange, too new,
Too unbelievable, too difficult,
Warring too much with common, easy ways . . .

Something is loosed to change the shaken world,
And with it we must change![1]

The lessons for the second Sunday of Advent begin with Isaiah's announcement of the Child-Messiah who will reorient our existence around God's vision of justice, righteousness, and peace. The Gospel takes us into the wilderness where John the Baptist confronts us with the dramatic reordering of our lives that will be required if we are to welcome the Son of God. Paul's words to the Romans describe life in the family of God that is reshaped around the life and love of Jesus Christ.

In the coming of this Son of God, something is loosed to change the shaken world. Advent is the time to realize the ways in which we must change.

THE NEWBORN KING
Isaiah 11:1-10

I am a vintage baby boomer, born in 1947. I well remember that blustery winter day when John F. Kennedy entered the White House with the promise that we were moving into "The New Frontier." There was a sense of hope-filled optimism in the realization that "the torch had been passed to a new generation." Almost anything seemed possible. We might even go to the moon! More recently, the same hope-filled optimism surrounded the release of Nelson Mandela from prison and the fall of the Berlin Wall. The emergence of new leadership embodied the possibility of a new alternative of freedom and justice for all.

That same kind of hope-filled optimism lies within the promise of Isaiah. The culture in which the prophet spoke was based on a "royal theology." The king embodied the covenant between God and Jerusalem. What happened to the king was a personification of what happened to the nation. The promise of a newborn king made almost anything seem possible.

In this passage Isaiah sees a new branch coming out of the "stump of Jesse." The stump is the image of humiliation, resignation, and defeat. People had good reason to think that the line of David was dead, lifeless, with no future and no hope. There seemed to be no alternative to the inevitable destruction and oppression that surrounded them.

But "prophetic imagination" enabled Isaiah to see God's alternative to the oppressive realities of the time. Isaiah announced the hope of a new branch growing out of the lifeless stump of Jesse. The new alternative that this Child-King would bring would be rooted in the past, but it would be energized by the Spirit of God to create a new future.

The unique character of the new king would be his relationship with God. "The spirit of the LORD shall rest on him" (11:2). The presence of the Spirit in his life would be expressed in "wisdom and understanding . . . counsel and might . . . knowledge and the fear of the LORD." These are clearly gifts of the Spirit in the life of the king, not unlike the gifts of the Spirit that Paul names in Galatians 5:22. They reflect the presence of God's Spirit in the central core of the human personality. These spiritual gifts express themselves in the down-to-earth, practical, social, and political realities with which the king has to deal, defined as righteousness and justice. The psalm for the day prescribed by the lectionary (Psalm 72) reinforces these themes as the defining core of divine kingship. Both themes, however, may need to be reclaimed and reinterpreted for our time.

Far too often the word *righteousness* brings to mind the narrow legalism and punctilious perfectionism of the Church Lady on "Saturday Night Live." *Justice* is too often seen as mere retribution for a crime. The biblical dimensions of those words go far beyond such narrow cultural definitions to penetrate the fabric of our daily lives.

Righteousness means "right-related-ness." It describes being in right relationship with God, right relationship with others, right relationship with the created order. It is the possibility of a life lived in balance with the creative purpose of God.

Biblical justice is God's right-related-ness in tangible form in the social, political, and economic arenas of human experience. It describes the ordering of life so that everyone gets exactly what they deserve as a part of God's human family, without the powerful taking advantage of the powerless or the strong oppressing the weak. God's justice is specifically measured in relationship to the welfare of the poor and the oppressed (Psalm 72:12-14).

Let's tell the truth. Aren't there times when the possibility of righteousness and justice in our world seems downright impossible? I can see rather clearly what it means to "get right with God" on a personal level through forgiveness and grace. Being in right relationship with others and with the world around us is another story.

The face of a particular person comes to mind. By our faith in Christ, both of us are in right relationship with God; but we are not in right relationship with each other. Now and then, particularly around Christmas, I make an attempt to heal that relationship. Most of the time, however, I do not expect anything to change. But then I remember a child in our congregation who has Downs' Syndrome and who sees every human being as a beautiful creation of God; and I wonder if Isaiah got it right. I wonder if a little child could lead us.

The Christmas season comes with its strange juxtaposition of a gift-buying orgy on one hand and the call for charitable giving on the other. I see the faces of children who receive so much more than they could ever use and children who receive so much less than they really need. Then I remember an elementary school boy who asked, "Why doesn't everyone just share what they have so everyone has enough?" And again I wonder if Isaiah got it right; perhaps a little child could lead us.

I revel in Isaiah's lyrical vision of the peaceable kingdom (Isaiah 11:6-9). It is a picture of life in the healed creation that seems utterly impossible in our "dog-eat-dog" world of competition and conflict. Then I remember that the task of a prophet is to hold before the people a visual image of possibilities the world often believes is impossible. I hear the angels sing, "Peace on earth and goodwill to all" this Advent season. Then I look at the child Jesus, the Branch from the root of Jesse, the Prince of Peace; and I'm quite sure Isaiah got it right. I am confident that *this* little Child can lead us.

How have you experienced the changes a child can bring?

What would it mean for you to be in right relationship with God? with others? with the world?

How could you reorient your life to live within the biblical vision of justice and peace?

THE WAY TO BETHLEHEM
Matthew 3:1-12

Ask the writers of the Gospels of Matthew, Mark, and Luke how to get to Bethlehem and they will give you the same directions. They are not so much directions that follow the geography of Palestine as directions that take us into the geography of the soul.

Frankly, it is not a journey I am all that excited about taking. It feels like a detour from the road marked with gifts to buy, cards to mail, a tree to decorate, and a turkey to stuff; but the Gospel writers take us this way each year on the second Sunday in Advent. They tell us to head out to the desert wilderness along the Jordan. When the going gets rough, turn to the right and look for a strange-looking man standing waist-deep in the water. He is dressed like an Old Testament prophet. His breath reeks of locusts and wild honey. And he is always preaching the same sermon: "Repent for the kingdom of heaven has come near." Ask the Gospel writers how to get to Bethlehem and they always send you to the wilderness to listen to John the Baptist.

John calls us to repent, to change the direction in which we are going. He challenges us to turn from our past and to move toward God's future. Turn from a narrow, self-centered existence, and move toward God's open-handed love. Turn from brokenness and bitterness, and move into God's healing and peace. Turn from self-destructive paths, and move into the way of life. Turn from the world's illusions of power, and reorder our life around the righteousness and justice of God. Turn from violence, and walk in the way of peace.

This turning, this repentance is a radical reorientation of our whole existence around the presence of the new-born Messiah-King in Bethlehem. Like parents "childproofing" their home, John calls us to clear things out, to make things straight, and to get ready for the coming of this Child to change our life. His life, death, and resurrection will be the fulfillment of Isaiah's vision. He will model the rule, will, and way of God in human flesh. Find that Child, and you will discover that

Something is loosed to change the shaken world,
And with it we must change![1]

I gave in during Advent and took the detour through the wilderness. I found John right where I expected him to be: soaked up to his middle in the river Jordan, his bony feet wrinkled by the water and turning blue, his face burned by the sun, and his hair blowing in the wind. I asked him the question I have wanted to ask before. "John," I blurted out, "Why can't you get into the Christmas spirit? Why do you insist on carping about repentance all the time? Cheer up, for heaven's sake! Drink some eggnog, decorate a tree, stand under the mistletoe, or watch a rerun of 'It's A Wonderful Life.' "

I knew that I had gone too far with that business about "It's A Wonderful Life." George Bailey, after all, nearly died before he turned things around. There's nothing like a hard, cold, wintery look at ourselves to reveal the need for repentance.

The water-logged prophet fixed his eyes on me. He looked down into a deeper place in my soul than I am generally willing to go. He found the neglected weeds and snarled undergrowth down there, and I began to feel his ax being laid to the root of my soul. He went to work on old habits, old attitudes, old prejudices that I needed to leave in the desert if I intended to go on to Bethlehem. He kept digging until he found broken places that needed healing, an old hurt, a bitter disappointment, a shattering defeat that I needed to leave in the past in order to claim God's future. He kept digging until he got to the roots of some old sins I should have uprooted long ago. I began to feel a fresh baptism of repentance cleaning out the deepest part of my personality, clearing a space in which the Son of God could once again be born.

There was a long, deep silence

MEET THE SON OF GOD

before I heard him say, "So, you want to see the new Child-King, do you?"

"You've got that right," I said. "I plan to be at the manger in about two weeks."

"And just what do you expect to find?" he asked.

"All the things Luke described," I said. "A baby wrapped in swaddling cloths, lying in a manger; shepherds keeping their flocks by night; and an angel saying, 'Do not be afraid; for see—I am bringing you good news of great joy.' "

"But you're following Matthew's directions this year," John replied. "What about Herod? What about the flight to Egypt? What about the threat this baby became to the existing order? Are you any more prepared for the changes this baby will bring than Herod was? I'm nothing compared to the One who is coming! Are you ready for his winnowing fork to go through your world?"

Just then I remembered the words of that innkeeper's wife:

Something is loosed to change the shaken world,
And with it we must change.[1]

I wondered just how well prepared I really was. Now I knew why the road to Bethlehem led through the wilderness.

Imagine yourself going to see John the Baptist in the wilderness. What would he find in you?

What will it mean for you to repent in preparation for the coming of the Son of God?

LIVING IN A NEW COMMUNITY
Romans 15:4-13

One of my all-time favorite Christmas stories was told by Garrison Keillor on National Public Radio's "A Prairie Home Companion" more than a decade ago. In "The News From Lake Wobegon," Keillor reported on the exiles who had come home for Christmas.

Corinne Ingqvist came home reluctantly, telling herself, "This soon shall pass." Lapsed Catholics returned to Our Lady of Perpetual Responsibility Church, where Father Emil poured on a rousing, John-the-Baptist-type sermon about their neglect of the faith that left them squirming in the pews. Eddie the Jealous Boy came home with his lovely wife Eunice, the most beautiful woman who had ever left Lake Wobegon. Foxy the Proud Boy arrived in his Ferlinghetti, a car that helped him forget his seedy roots. And Larry the Sad Boy, who had been saved twelve times at the Lutheran Church, came back for one more round of penance. They were all there, Keillor said, drawn by the strange power that Christmas exerts in all of us, the magnetic power that draws us close to people we love. (You will find this story in *Leaving Home: A Collection of Lake Wobegon Stories*.)

Babies exert magnetic power upon us too. Relatives from around the country had gathered in Seattle to welcome our newly-adopted infant nephew into the family. We had chosen a seafood restaurant looking out across Puget Sound. Three generations of adults were engaged in intelligent conversation until the baby arrived. Suddenly, all other conversation seemed irrelevant. The center of gravity shifted. Each one of us was drawn to the innocence, simplicity, and gurgling presence of that child.

In the Epistle lesson Paul outlines the practical implications of the magnetic power of the love of God that draws us together in the body of Christ. The church is called to model the new alternative of life under the rule of the Prince of Peace. Our fellowship is intended to be the magnetic center in which people are drawn together in shared strength, celebrative praise, and joy-filled hope.

Romans 15:1-13 is organized around two direct commands (verses 1-2, 7), each of which is followed by a wish or prayer (verses 5-6, 13). First, Paul says that "we who are strong ought to put up with the failings of the weak" (Romans 15:1). Paul's command grows out of the deep conviction that "we do not live to ourselves, and we do not die to ourselves" (14:7). The goal of each member of the body is to "pursue what makes for peace and for mutual upbuilding" (14:19). The apostle calls us to serve, support, encourage, and build each other up, just the way Christ served us.

Dietrich Bonhoeffer, writing from a Nazi prison cell, said that "we must learn to regard people less in the light of what they do or omit to do, and more in the light of what they suffer. The only profitable relationship to others—and especially to our weaker brethren —is one of love."[2]

This calling results in Paul's prayerful hope in Romans 15:5-6 that "the God of steadfastness and encouragement grant you to live in harmony with one another, in accordance with Christ Jesus, so that together you may with one voice glorify the God and Father of our Lord Jesus Christ." An essential characteristic of the new alternative of life in the Christian community is that the strong use their strength to build up the weak, resulting in a song of united praise to God.

Paul also commands us to "welcome one another, therefore, just as Christ has welcomed [us]." The radical nature of this Christ-like welcome is expressed in Eugene Peterson's paraphrase of one of the Old Testament verses that Paul quotes in the passage.

Then I'll join outsiders in a hymn-song;
I'll sing your name! . . .
Outsiders and insiders, rejoice together! . . .
People of all nations, celebrate God!
All colors and races, give hearty praise![3]

There is a shocking inclusiveness in the way Christ welcomes us into the family of God, an inclusiveness that breaks through all the barriers of age, sex, race, nationality, and culture that the world builds around us. We are called to offer the same kind of welcome to everyone who is drawn toward us in the love of God. It is a "come to the party" sort of welcome that rejoices in the simple presence of each grace-invited guest.

This glad-hearted welcome results in Paul's prayerful hope in verse 13: "May the God of hope fill you with all joy and peace in believing, so that you may abound in hope by the power of the Holy Spirit." The welcome that we extend to others in the Christian family is a sign of hope that results in great joy and peace.

Within his first Advent days in the monastery, Thomas Merton discovered what became one of the most important aspects of his life as a monk. "The first and most elementary test of one's call . . . is the willingness to accept life in a community in which everybody is more or less imperfect."[4] He acknowledged that the imperfections of the monks were, by and large, much more trivial than the vices of people in the world; and yet, they seemed to be magnified by the ideal vision of monastic life. But as he settled into life among the brothers, he experienced a growing acceptance of others' imperfections. He found a genuine enthusiasm that expressed itself in ingenious good humor. In the monastery Merton experienced the child-like changes that his new life in Christ would bring.

If we fully experience it, Advent is a time to face up to the changes this Child-King of Bethlehem brings. It is a time for us to allow our lives to be reoriented around the presence of this Son of God so that we become the living expression of God's love and our churches become the present witness to God's righteousness, justice, and peace.

Something is loosed to change the shaken world,
And with it we must change![1]

How have you seen or experienced the building up of each other in the fellowship of the church?

What changes need to be made for Romans 15:5-6 to become a reality in your congregation?

Stupendous height of heavenly love,
Of pitying tenderness divine!
It brought the Saviour from above,
It caused the springing day to shine;
The Sun of righteousness to appear,
And gild our gloomy hemisphere.

God did in Christ himself reveal,
To chase our darkness by his light,

Our sin and ignorance dispel,
   Direct our wandering feet
aright,
And bring our souls, with pardon
blest,
   To realms of everlasting rest.

Answer thy mercy's whole design,
   My God incarnated for me;
My spirit make thy radiant shrine,
   My light and full salvation be,
And through the shades of death
unknown
   Conduct me to thy dazzling
throne.[5]

                    Charles Wesley

[1] From *A Child Is Born,* by Stephen Vincent Benet (Walter H. Baker Company, 1942); pages 24-25.
[2] From *Letters and Papers From Prison,* by Dietrich Bonhoeffer (The MacMillan Company, 1953), page 9.
[3] Scripture taken from *The Message.* Copyright © by Eugene H. Peterson, 1993, 1994, 1995, 1996. Used by permission of NavPress Publishing Group.
[4] From *A Thomas Merton Reader,* edited by Thomas P. McDonnell (Image Books Doubleday, 1974); page 153.
[5] From *Wesley Hymns,* compiled by Ken Bible (Lillenas Publishing, Co., 1982); no. 145.

An Explosion of Joy

Scriptures for Advent: The Third Sunday
Isaiah 35
Matthew 11:2-11
James 5:7-10

Thomas Merton's phrase snagged my attention just the way he intended when he had it printed in bold type.

When . . . the joy which is **The Great Joy,** explodes silently upon the world, there is no longer any room for sadness. . . . No circumstance . . . however trivial . . . is to be left out of The Great Joy. In the special and heavenly light which shines around the coming of the Word into the world, all ordinary things are transfigured.[1]

Read that paragraph again. Allow Merton's words to sink into your soul as you prepare to receive **The Great Joy**.

The third Sunday in Advent is called *Gaudete,* the Latin word for "Rejoice!" from the traditional Roman Catholic introit for the day. The use of a pink candle in the Advent wreath represents this rejoicing. The setting aside of a day of rejoicing is drawn from an old Roman practice of observing the fourth Sunday in Lent as a time of rejoicing in that long, somber season of repentance. Similarly, the third Sunday in Advent celebrates the joy of our hope during the otherwise restrained observance of Advent.

The explosion of joy in this year's lectionary readings begins with Isaiah's vision of God's intervention in a world under the influence of disabling dryness and death. In the Gospel, the haunting question of John the Baptist is answered by the description of the life-giving difference Jesus has been making in people's lives. The epistle calls us to patience as we await the fulfillment of God's healing alternative in the coming of the Lord.

The explosion of joy for which we long and wait is nothing less than the intrusion of God's life, God's wholeness, and God's healing power in the real lives of real people and the real world in which we live. Now and then we see the evidence of this divine intrusion into human experiences, and it is enough to fill our life with joy.

A woman came to see me the week before Christmas. We looked back over the two years since, in her words, she dragged herself into the church. For more than a decade she had rejected organized religion, but Christmas had drawn her back. The first time she came to see me, she was suffering from a rare neuromuscular disorder. She had read one of my books and said she was ready for war. She did not understand why God would need to come to save her. She was surprised when I did not kick her out or argue the theology of the Incarnation. I said she was in good company in that faithful Christian people have had a hard time understanding the Incarnation for two thousand years, but they keep on experiencing it anyway.

She kept coming to worship. She joined a DISCIPLE Bible study group. An amazing transformation began to take place in her life. She was healed of her muscular disorder. She called what she had experienced "a transfusion of love." She said, "This church helped me get on the highway to God."

The prophetic imagination of Advent invites each of us to journey on the highway to God. It is the pathway of exploding joy!

THE SENSUOUS SEASON
Isaiah 35

The Christmas season engages all our senses. During Advent, I look forward to *seeing* the lights on the tree, *hearing* the carols, *smelling* my mother's steam pudding on the stove, *feeling* a chill in the air (Yes, even in Tampa!), and *tasting* ornament-shaped sugar cookies with colored frosting. It is a sensuous season during which I allow every part of my being to take in the gifts of love and joy.

The prophetic vision in Isaiah 35 is surprisingly sensuous. Before we *say* anything about it, we need to *see* it by allowing the images to form in our imagination. *Taste* the dusty dryness of the desert. *Hear* the rain pattering on the barren ground. *Smell* the earth as it drinks in the life-giving moisture. *Watch* the crocus burst open, the dry grass become reeds and rushes in the watery marsh. *Listen* for the green sounds of the earth breaking forth in singing. *Imagine* the darkness of eyes that cannot see, the silence of ears that cannot hear. *Feel* the imprisonment of paralyzed limbs that cannot move, the shaking knees of people filled with fear. *Sense* the arrival of a power strong enough to open blind eyes, to unplug deaf ears, and to energize weak limbs to leap and dance. *Hear* the power that can cause speechless tongues to sing and shout for joy.

Having experienced the vision,

we are prepared to study it more closely. The opening verses of the poem have a "chiastic" structure. The order of the images in the first section are reversed in the second:

(a) Verses 1-2: healing for the earth
(b) Verse 3: healing strength for disabled humanity
(c) Verse 4: the coming of God
(b') Verses 5-6a: healing strength for disabled humanity
(a') Verses 6b-7: healing for the earth.

The prevailing condition of the creation is arid drought, a common experience for the desert dwellers of the Middle East. The prevailing condition of humanity is that people are disabled. They are unable to experience the fullness of life either due to actual physical disabilities or to the disabling power of fear, oppression, or sorrow. The chiastic hinge that reverses the flow of those life-limiting forces is in verse 4: "Here is your God . . . . He will come and save you."

The life of human beings and the life of the earth are renewed by the intervention of God's healing, restoring, life-giving presence. It is not the result of life-forces that human beings or the earth have within themselves. It is the result of God's infusion of life from the outside.

In 1943, Dietrich Bonhoeffer compared Advent to his experience in a Nazi prison cell. "One waits, hopes, and does this, that, or the other—things that are really of no consequence—the door is shut, and can be opened only *from the outside*."[2] (The italics are Bonhoeffer's.)

The great good news of the prophetic vision is that God comes *from the outside* with salvation for the whole creation. Biblical salvation is not simply making individual reservations in heaven for our souls after death. Salvation involves the healing and empowering of life in the present to fulfill God's vision for the future. God saves us by healing the brokenness in our lives and by restoring the life of the earth. Shakespeare described the saving impact of Christ's birth in these lines from *Hamlet*:

Some say that ever 'gainst that season comes
Wherein our Saviour's birth is celebrated,
The bird of dawning singeth all night long:
And then, they say, no spirit dare stir abroad;
The nights are wholesome; then no planets strike,
No fairy takes, nor witch hath power to charm,
So hallow'd and so gracious is the time. (Act I, Scene 1)

The result of God's intrusion into human history is that weak hands are strengthened, wobbly knees are made firm, and the whole created order shares the joy of new life.

I grew up in a tradition in which teenagers who were tempted to square dance or do the "jitterbug" were encouraged to read a book entitled *From the Ballroom to Hell.* Throughout the Old Testament, however, dancing is the response of the whole being to the goodness of life and the joy of God's presence. When God's salvation comes, you can feel it in your toes.

God's healing alternative strengthens weak limbs to walk and dance with joy on the highway, the Holy Way, of God. The prophet promises that "no traveler, not even fools, shall go astray," which I take as good news for all those male drivers—like myself—who refuse to ask for directions.

In verses 9 and 10, the prophet envisions a joyful procession to Zion:

The redeemed shall walk there.
And the ransomed of the LORD shall return,
  and come to Zion with singing;
everlasting joy shall be upon their heads;
  they shall obtain joy and gladness,
  and sorrow and sighing shall flee away.

This is Isaiah's vision of the exiles making their way back to Jerusalem, but it is also a picture of the road we travel during Advent. Our journey is filled with joy, the kind of joy that strengthens weak hands and tired knees; the kind of joy that puts a new song in your mouth and new rhythm in your feet. The kind of joy that comes from the same place as tears.

We are talking about divine intervention: nothing short of a transfusion of divine life into the old order, the old assumptions, the barren and tragic business as usual of a broken, hurting world. It is the joy that comes because of the infusion of God's life-giving presence in the desert of our souls. Walter Brueggemann called this poem "a healing alternative to the church's grim despair and to our modern sense that no real newness is possible."[3] We are invited out of our carefully managed rationality to celebrate the way God does what the world would think is impossible. "Advent," Brueggemann said, "is getting ready for that impossibility which will permit us to dance and sing and march and thank and drink—and live!"[4]

The astounding good news we proclaim at Christmas is that God has acted in human history. In this single event, one moment in time, all the love and life of God was molded into human flesh and came forth from the womb of Mary as a baby in a manger. We dare proclaim that this Jesus was exactly who the Gospels say he was, "Immanuel," which means "God with us."

How does Christmas engage your senses? How do your senses respond to the images in Isaiah's vision?

How have you experienced God's healing alternative in your life?

What does it mean for you to hear the words, "Here is your God. . . . He will come and save you"?

ARE YOU THE ONE?
Matthew 11:2-11

John the Baptist, in prison and not likely to get out with his head, sent a haunting question to Jesus through his followers: "Are you the one who is to come, or are we to wait for another?" And inquiring minds all want to know: What's going on here? Just last Sunday we heard the wilderness-shaking voice of this prophet announcing the coming of Christ with a confidence that rattled the trees and shattered the pious pretensions of our lives. How can the same person now ask this kind of question?

Scholars, preachers, and amateur psychologists generally offer two responses. One is a "contextual" response: John is in prison. The prophet whose life was shaped in the wild freedom of the wilderness, with the wind in his hair, the sun on his back, and the sounds and smells of the earth saturating his soul, is now confined in the dark, stinking, narrow cell of Herod's prison. Before his life ends, he must have some assurance, some clear-cut evidence that his life was not wasted and that the promise has been fulfilled. Like Bonhoeffer, he waits for a word to confirm God's intervention *from the outside.*

The other response is "textual," pointing directly to verse 2: "John heard in prison what the Messiah was doing." Matthew 8–9 gives us the composite picture of what Jesus was doing: healing lepers, raising a paralyzed servant, calming a storm, releasing people from the power of demons, feasting with tax collectors and sinners, and restoring sight to the blind. Matthew summarizes Jesus' actions in 9:36: "When he saw the crowds, he had compassion for them, because they were harassed and helpless, like sheep without a shepherd."

If that was what John had been hearing about Jesus, he could have good reason for his question. It does not have quite the same ring as John's call to "flee from the wrath to come." It does not look like an ax being laid to the root of a tree with barren branches being thrown into the fire. It is hard to picture this Messiah clearing the thrashing floor with his pitchfork (Matthew 3:7-12). The means by which Jesus had been fulfilling the messianic promise were not exactly consistent with John's expectations. As great as John was, he still shared a vision of reality that assumed that the kingdom of heaven would come through some form of violence and force (11:12). After hearing what Jesus was doing, John had no alternative but to ask, "Are you the one?"

Jesus' response clarifies the way in which he is the fulfillment of the prophetic vision. First, Jesus points to the things John's disciples were hearing and seeing. God's saving presence in Jesus is identified, not in prophetic words, but in prophetic action. He is the personal fulfill-ment of Isaiah's vision as the heal-ing, life-giving, saving presence of God.

Second, Jesus clarifies his messiah-ship by laying claim to specific parts of the prophetic vision in Isaiah 29:18-19; 35:5-6; and 61:1-4. These form the central core of his ministry. There is judgment in Jesus, to be sure; but it is judgment revealed through healing, judg-ment against all that keeps this cre-ated order from the fullness of life God intends. Jesus does not save the world by destroying it but by renewing it in the life God intended. Realizing that his way of fulfilling God's vision will be hard for some folks to accept, Jesus pronounces his blessing on anyone who is able to receive this kind of messiahship without being overwhelmed by it (Matthew 11:6).

John's struggle is our own. His question raises the difficulty we have with this Jesus who relentlessly refuses to use what the world calls power to fulfill the promise of the rule and reign of God. Jesus is the continuing contradiction of the "Star Wars" mentality of the good guys who finally win by beating up on the bad guys with the same destructive power that evil uses against them. The power of God's saving presence in Jesus does not destroy but heals. God in Christ defeats death, not with more death, but with life. God defeats hatred, not with more hatred, but with love. God wins the victory, not by destroying the bad guys, but by

transforming enemies into friends (2 Corinthians 5).

The difficulty is that we have been conditioned to march to the drumbeat of the world's systems of power and force. We have a hard time learning to dance to the music of the Kingdom. Although it is not part of the lectionary read-ing, later on in this passage Jesus compares the response of the peo-ple who hear and see him to chil-dren in the marketplace. In verse 17, he quotes what was evidently a familiar little ditty of that day:

We played the flute for you, and you did not dance;
    we wailed and you did not mourn.

Some folks refuse to get into the rhythm of the music. John came as the vigorous voice of forceful repentance, pointing out the bad news of sin; and he was written off as having a demon. The Son of Man came eating and drinking, bringing the joy of the Kingdom, celebrating the healing life and joy of God's salvation; and he was called a glutton. Yet wisdom is vin-dicated by her deeds. In other words, what you see is what you get. If there is music in the air, why aren't you dancing? Will we receive the gift of new life God brings to us in Jesus Christ, the Son of God?

When have you felt like John? When have you asked, "Are you the one?"

If you were John, how would you

have responded to the answer Jesus sent back?

The eternal God from heaven
    came down,
The King of glory dropped his
    crown,
And veiled his majesty;
Emptied of all but love he came,
Jesus, I call thee by the name,
Thy pity bore for me.

In my weak, sinful flesh appear;
O God, be manifested here,
Peace, righteousness and joy;
Thy kingdom, Lord, set up within,
My faithful heart; and all my sin,
The devil's work destroy.[5]

Charles Wesley

THE PATIENCE OF THE PROPHETS
James 5:7-10

One of the last places you would probably go to look for Christmas joy would be to a prison. As Dietrich Bonhoeffer prepared for Christmas in his prison cell, he acknowledged that "in view of all the misery that prevails here, anything like a prctty-pretty, sentimental reminder of Christmas is out of place."[6]

For Bonhoeffer, imprisonment forced a soul-level evaluation of himself and his faith. He could have remained safe in the United States, but he chose to return to Germany to join the witness against Hitler. Looking back on that decision, he said, "I want to assure you that I have not for a moment regretted coming back in 1939—nor any of the consequences, either. I knew quite well what I was doing, and I acted with a clear conscience. . . . All we can do is to live in assurance and faith—you out there with the soldiers, and I in my cell."[7]

And yet, it was in that same cell that he wrote of *hilaritas* (serenity) as a central part of genuine greatness. People who experience *hilaritas* have a basic "steadfast certainty that in their own work they are showing the world something *good* (even if the world does not like it), and a high-spirited self-confidence."[8] He affirmed the source of that confidence in his personal creed:

I believe that God can and will bring good out of evil, even out of the greatest evil. . . . I believe that God will give us all the strength we need to help us to resist in time of distress. But he never gives it in advance, lest we should rely on ourselves and not on him alone. A faith such as this should allay all our fears of the future.[9]

Dietrich Bonhoeffer is a twentieth century example of the kind of faith to which the Epistle of James calls us. The epistle is addressed to "the twelve tribes in the Dispersion." *Diaspora* was the technical term to describe Jews who lived outside Palestine, generally exiles and refugees, fleeing oppression and persecution. The writer used that image as a metaphor for the members of the early church who felt like aliens in a foreign culture. The Epistle of James is a practical letter intended to guide believers in maintaining their identity in a world that does not understand and often rejects the claims of the gospel. The concluding paragraphs are a word of encouragement for those who are tempted to give up on the hope of God's healing alternative becoming a reality in this world.

Hopeful living calls for patience. This patience is not passive acquiescence, but it is patience as active confidence in the promise of God; this patience grows out of absolute assurance in the final coming of the Lord.

The writer offers two examples of this kind of patience. One is the patience of farmers who plant their crops and wait for the coming rain. This example takes us back to the powerful imagery with which Isaiah described the promise of God's healing alternative for the world. Faithful patience is rooted in absolute confidence in the God who promises to fulfill the prophetic vision of the healing of the whole created order.

The second example of patience is that of the biblical prophets who spoke out of their suffering. One of the great paradoxes of the prophetic tradition is that the word of hope and joy always emerges out of the same place as suffering. The biblical prophets were, to use W. H. Auden's description of William Butler Yeats, "hurt into poetry."

Real pain and real joy emerge from the same depths of the human soul. Only those who know the tears of great pain can know the laughter of profound joy.

As Christmas 1943 approached, Deitrich Bonhoeffer wrote a letter to his brother who was on the front lines. He wondered how and where the two of them would celebrate Christmas that year. Then he offered this word of encouragement:

I hope you will manage to communicate something of its joy . . . to your fellow soldiers. For the calmness and joy with which we meet what is laid on us are as infectious as the terror that I see among the people here at each new attack. . . We are neither of us daredevils, but that has nothing to do with the courage that comes from the grace of God.[10]

I will never forget her face, although twenty-six years later I cannot remember her name. It was my first Christmas Eve in the first church I served. During the weeks of Advent, I had walked with her through more pain than I can fully remember. She had been diagnosed with cancer. Her husband had walked out on her. There had been a death in the extended family. She had lost her job. Her life, by the world's standards, was an absolute wreck.

But I still remember her face. As I processed with the choir to the singing of "O Come All Ye

Faithful," I saw her, seated in the first row. As we turned to face the congregation, I saw the tears that gushed from her eyes and ran down over her face. But as I looked into her eyes, I became powerfully aware that they were not tears of pain, frustration, discouragement, or defeat. It was obvious that they were tears of unexpected, soul-level joy! This joy was deeper than mere happiness and stronger than pain. **The Great Joy** was silently exploding from within the depths of her soul.

I see people like her every year. These are people who make their way into the sanctuary on Christmas Eve with hesitating steps because they are coming alone for the first time. The empty seat beside them is a mute witness to the painful loss they have experienced. They come having faced great defeat, soul-shattering loss, and disabling pain. Yet they come expecting that the same God who brought new life to the desert will bring new life to their parched and drought-stricken souls. The same God who brought strength to feeble limbs will bring strength for them to face the future. The same God whose healing alternative for the world was revealed in the events John's disciples observed will bring healing for their lives. They come with patient expectation that the seeds of trust and faith they have planted will grow into an abundant crop. They come in patient expectation that just as God brought hope out of the suffering of the prophets, God will bring joy out of their pain.

I watch in amazement as I see **The Great Joy** exploding silently in their lives. They are not naive or overly sentimental about reality; but no circumstance, however trivial, is left out. In the heavenly light that shines around them as they hear the Christmas story, "all ordinary things are transfigured."

Year after year, I see the promise of Isaiah's vision fulfilled. The ransomed of the Lord return. They come with singing and in the realization that in the Baby of Bethlehem, God has come to save them. They "obtain joy and gladness, and sorrow and sighing . . . flee away."

How have you observed the kind of patience James describes?

When have you felt the joy that emerges from pain?

Have you experienced a Christmas Eve like the one described here? How was your pain turned into joy?

[1] From *A Thomas Merton Reader;* page 360.
[2] From *Letters and Papers From Prison;* page 78.
[3] From *Texts for Preaching,* Walter Brueggemann, Charles B. Cousar, Beverly R. Gaventa, James D. Newsome (Westminster John Knox Press, 1995); page 21.
[4] From *Texts for Preaching;* page 21.
[5] From *Christian Year and Occasional Hymns;* page 45.
[6] From *Letters and Papers From Prison;* page 97.
[7] From *Letters and Papers From Prison;* page 99.
[8] From *Letters and Papers From Prison;* page 123.
[9] From *Letters and Papers From Prison;* page 11.
[10] From *Letters and Papers From Prison;* pages 85-86.

"God Contracted to a Span"

Thomas Merton entered the silence of a Trappist monastery during Advent, but the grace of God that brought him there began on the noisy streets of New York City. Reflecting on his life, he concluded that "all our salvation begins on the level of common and natural and ordinary things."[1]

The mystery and glory of the gospel is that common, natural, ordinary things become the means by which God intersects our human experience with the healing alternative of salvation. God meets us in places as common as a small-town stable. God announces "good news of great joy" to people who are as ordinary as shepherds watching their flocks. God comes to be with us through the birth of a child, the most supernaturally natural experience in human life. God uses natural things —baptismal water and Communion bread and wine—as the supernatural gifts of sacramental grace.

In the Old Testament lesson we find King Ahaz frozen with fear in a city under siege. Isaiah announces the promise of a prophetic sign from God: a child who will bear the name "Immanuel." That child will be the ever-present reminder of the presence of God. Matthew takes us into the conflicted soul of Joseph as he responds to the shocking news that Mary is pregnant. Matthew interprets the event in light of Isaiah's child-sign; but looking back from this side of the Resurrection, he goes beyond Isaiah to declare that Jesus is the tangible, flesh-and-blood, incarnate presence of God with us. The epistle to Rome opens with the bold affirmation that Jesus is totally human—"descended from David according to the flesh"—and fully divine—"declared to be Son of God with power according to the spirit of holiness." The texts draw us into the incomprehensible mystery of what Paul calls "the gospel of God," the good news of God's salvation in common, natural, and ordinary human flesh.

The God who comes to us in the birth of Jesus is not the *deus ex machina* of Greek and Roman tragedy, a convenient but artificially-contrived god who drops in from the sky in the final act to resolve all the complex difficulties that have gone before. The doctrine of the Incarnation proclaims the coming of God to be one of us, one with us, all the way from conception to birth, through life and death, and into life everlasting. The good news of Christmas goes beyond our human comprehension and calls us to the deep, inner obedience of faith.

One of Charles Wesley's greatest carols has not appeared in American hymnals for more than one hundred years. The verses of that carol will serve as a connecting thread for this chapter.

Let earth and heaven combine,
    Angels and men agree,
To praise in songs divine
    The incarnate Deity,
Our God contracted to a span,
    Incomprehensibly made man.[2]

"THE MILD IMMANUEL'S NAME"
Isaiah 7:10-16

In the fall of 1937, reports of Nazi violence and oppression in Europe cast ominous shadows across the Atlantic Ocean. Thomas Merton was a journalism student at Columbia University. He described the amazing ways in which God acted to "rescue us from the confusion and the misery in which we had come to find ourselves, partly through our own fault, and partly through a complex set of circumstances"[3] His words are a powerful description of what the Bible means by salvation. Merton said that friendship, books, ideas, poetry, art, anxiety about war and injustice, even the noisy streets and aging buildings of New York City, became the instruments through which God's grace intersected with his life and brought salvation.

It was in a similar time and manner that God acted in the life of King Ahaz of Judah, eight centuries before the birth of Christ. Israel and Syria had formed a coalition to fight against Assyria, the military superpower of the day. Ahaz had not joined the coalition, which weakened its chances of success and led Israel and Syria to attack Judah, laying siege to the city of Jerusalem. No wonder "the heart of Ahaz and the heart of his people shook as the trees of the forest shake before the wind" (Isaiah 7:2).

For Jerusalem, the military crisis on the outside provoked a theological crisis on the inside. God's promise to be with the covenant people took tangible form in the Temple. The king was called to lead the nation on the basis of his relationship with God, but Ahaz's faith had been shattered by the circumstances surrounding him. Under siege by military forces without and spiritual anxiety within,

Ahaz desperately needed the word he received from Isaiah: "Take heed, be quiet, do not fear, and do not let your heart be faint" (verse 4).

But God's promise was more than Ahaz could believe. Our reading begins with the Lord's astonishing offer to Ahaz: "Ask a sign of the LORD your God; let it be deep as Sheol or high as heaven." It is a shocking moment of divine condescension. The Almighty God offers to come to Ahaz in common, ordinary, natural things. Ahaz responds with mock humility, which fails to hide his lack of faith. "Oh, not me! I'd never stoop so low as to put God to a test!" Isaiah's response reveals unmistakable frustration: "It's bad enough for you to wear out the patience of men—do you have to wear out God's patience too?" (7:13, *Today's English Version*).

The Lord shattered Ahaz's artificial piety by declaring that whether he wanted it or not, he would get a sign. "Look, the young woman is with child and shall bear a son, and shall name him Immanuel." Every time Ahaz heard that royal baby cry or watched that royal child running around the royal palace, he would be reminded that God's presence was just as real as the presence of that child.

Have you noticed how a baby's name can be a reminder of someone else? Perhaps that is why I have never known parents to name their son Ebenezer. I am named for an uncle whose plane was shot down over Holland in World War II. He was one of those young pilots whose story was told in the movie "Memphis Belle." I never knew Uncle Jim, except to see his face in fading family pictures or to hear the legend of his laughter in a family that was infected with congenital seriousness. But every time I sign a Christmas card, it is a continuing reminder of his presence in our family identity.

This child named Immanuel would be the constant reminder of the presence of God. In a city under siege, the birth of this child would be the sign of new life. In a situation of destruction and death, this child would be the sign of hope, of "such days as have not come since the day that Ephraim departed from Judah." Here was the promise of a future greater than the halycon days before the dividing of the kingdom into Ephraim (Israel) in the north and Judah in the south.

Stephen Speilberg's historical epic "Amistad" is the true story of a shipload of kidnapped Africans who spent two years in the United States until the Supreme Court declared them to be free people and sent them back to Sierra Leone. In the agony of the slave ship a baby is born. As that newborn child is lifted above the writhing bodies of the chained slaves, it becomes a tangible expression of hope in a hopeless situation. It is lifted up as a sign of life in the midst of death.

Merton said that one of his Columbia friends was always waiting for a "sign" that he defined as "some . . . sensible and tangible interior jolt from God, to get him started." The problem was that while he waited, "he did all the things that normally exclude and nullify the action of grace."[4] What about each of us?

Are you waiting for a sign?

What have you done to prepare yourself to receive that sign? What have you done that could exclude and nullify the action of grace?

What common, ordinary, natural signs have you received that you would name "Immanuel" in your experience?

He laid his glory by,
He wrappéd him in our clay,
Unmarkéd by human eye,
The latent Godhead lay,
Infant of days he here became;
And bore the mild Immanuel's name.[5]

"HE DEIGNS IN FLESH TO APPEAR"
Matthew 1:18-25

Thomas Merton remembered a November day when a friend recommended a book that opened his life to the possibility of a supernatural order that was immediately accessible and could be reached by prayer, faith, and love. Other books, conversations, and experiences prepared him to attend his first mass at the Church of Corpus Christi on 121st Street in New York City. Inexperienced in attending church, he found his way to an obscure corner of the sanctuary. As he listened to a young priest's sermon, he sensed that for the people gathered around him all this was a familiar and integrated part of their lives.

The priest said that Christ was the Son of God. He was not simply a man, a good man, or even a great prophet, but something more, something that made everything else seem trivial and irrelevant. He was God. But he was also human, born of flesh and blood. This Christ was God present with us in human flesh; and as such, he loved us, suffered for us, died for us, and was raised to new life. Then the priest went one step further, declaring that as mysterious as it all is, if you believe it, you will receive light enough to understand it. But if you wait to fully understand it, you will never believe it.

Merton said the sermon was exactly what he needed. Here is his lyrical description of how he felt as he left the church that day.

I walked leisurely down Broadway in the sun, and my eyes looked about me at a new world. I could not understand . . . why I was so much at peace, so content with life for I was not yet used to the clean savor that comes with an actual grace. . . . All I know is that I walked in a new world.[6]

The paralyzing siege of confusion and doubt was broken. He

had entered into a new world, and everything was transfigured by it.

I wonder if something like that might have happened for Joseph. Like Ahaz, Joseph was a man in crisis. His soul was under siege. Matthew says he was a righteous man, a good man in the best sense of the word. His first thought was to dissolve the engagement without disgracing Mary. But what would he do? And where was God in all of this?

Joseph received the same word Isaiah brought to Ahaz: "Do not be afraid." It is the standard greeting for every angel in the nativity story. Joseph heard the angel's words in the dark night of his soul: "Joseph, son of David, do not be afraid to take Mary as your wife, for the child conceived in her is from the Holy Spirit."

This supernatural announcement must have been just about as confusing as it was helpful. It marked an extraordinary intervention of God's saving presence in the natural, ordinary stuff of human experience; but it had to be totally beyond Joseph's rational understanding.

A fellow pastor described a fifteenth century painting of *The Visitation of the Shepherds* by Ghirlandaio, which hangs in the Church of the Holy Trinity in Florence, Italy. All the nativity characters are there. Mary clasps her hands over the child in prayer. Shepherds kneel in adoration. A long procession of people winds its way toward the manger. Everyone is looking at the Christ Child, including the animals. Everyone is looking except Joseph. He stands in the shadows, gazing up at an angel and scratching his head. Assuming that scratching your head meant the same thing in the fifteenth century as it does today, the artist is suggesting that Joseph was still trying to figure all this out.

I'm certain that Joseph did not understand the virgin birth any better than we do. But Joseph knew, in a place where knowing goes deeper than rational thought, that God had intersected human history in the birth of this child. That night when the angel came to him in a dream, he stepped into a new world. The road ahead would be filled with risk, pain, and an utter inability to fully explain how it had all happened; but he must have known the inner peace of what Merton called "the clean savor that comes with an actual grace."

"You are to name him Jesus," the angel said, "for he will save his people from their sins." And that is exactly what Joseph did: "He did as the angel of the Lord commanded him . . . he named him Jesus" (1:25). Joseph acted in faithful obedience and became the first person to declare the unique identity of Mary's son. Although he had no way of knowing how it would happen (how could he have imagined the cross and the Resurrection?), he knew that if there was any hope of salvation for a sinful, broken, confused world, it would be found in this child whom he named Jesus.

Matthew interprets the theological significance of this birth by recognizing the Isaiah passage as a bold declaration that this child born of the virgin Mary is more than just the "sign" of God's presence; Jesus literally *is* God with us. This baby is "God contracted to a span/Incomprehensibly made man." We dare to affirm that from the very beginning of his life, Jesus was the living demonstration of the essential character of the Almighty God. There was no part of his existence not animated by the Spirit of God.

With the birth of this child, we enter a new world. There are mysteries of God's invasion of human history that we must believe if we ever hope to understand. If we wait for complete understanding, we will never believe. When we respond with believing obedience, we move beyond cognitive understanding to a depth of knowing that goes all the way to the bottom of our souls. But the process of believing obedience may not be any easier for us than it was for Joseph.

As I was preparing for the first Sunday in Advent, I received a letter from a pastor/brother in South Africa who shared his own struggle with the mystery of the Incarnation. He described Advent as "a time of deep introspection" that led him to question just how deeply he actually believed. He said, "I know Jesus the person, but sometimes I wonder if I know Jesus the God. Jesus for me is fully human, but sometimes I question the reality of his living power in my life . . . I just do not seem to allow that side of him to take hold of me. . . . I almost feel that I am holding back—that I have not abandoned my life, my all, into God's hands."

This man knew enough to know that he would never fully believe until he had obeyed. He would never know the fullness of God's presence in Jesus until he had abandoned his life into God's hands.

When I read his letter, I pictured Joseph, standing in the shadows of the manger, scratching his head. Joseph was still amazed, still wondering, but still there. He was faithful, obedient, and ready to be the person to name this child Jesus and to claim him as the one who would save people from their sins.

When have you felt that your soul was under siege?

How has "believing obedience" led toward "understanding" for you?

How are you "holding back" from abandoning your life into God's hands?

Unsearchable the love,
    That hath the Saviour brought,
The grace is far above,
    Or man or angel's thought:
Suffice for us that God we know,
Our God is manifest below. [7]

"WIDEST EXTREMES TO JOIN"

Romans 1:1-7

A fellow pastor and friend shared with me the way the Spirit of God has been helping him define the difference between those things at the center and those at the boundaries of the life of faith. Too often, he said, we spend our energy fighting or fretting over boundary issues, things out on the edges of life, instead of allowing the Spirit of God to move into the central core of our experience. The challenge is to allow the Spirit to take us deeper and deeper into the center, which means allowing the Spirit of God to reorient our personality around the love of God in Jesus Christ.

Paul had never met the Christians in Rome, so he began this letter at the central core of their common faith in Christ. He defined the energizing nucleus of the Christian life in three movements, beginning with what he called "the gospel of God," literally, "God's gospel."

We need to be reminded that the good news we declare does not belong to us. It was not produced, designed, or invented out of our human ingenuity. It is not a religious commodity over which we have control. The good news of salvation is the story of God's action, and it is under God's control.

During Advent, we face the very real danger that the warmth, senti-mentality, and beauty of our Christmas traditions will tempt us to handle the gospel like a family heirloom ornament we unwrap and hang on the tree each year. The story of the baby in the manger becomes a cozy tale told by warm candlelight glow with a yule log crackling in a comfy fireplace. Mary and Joseph become little more than pious, plaster figurines that can be safely packed away when the holidays are over.

But if the story we tell is "God's gospel," it is not something we unpack nearly so much as it is God's power to unpack us, to strip us of our pretentious pride, and to hang our souls out in the clear light of divine grace. If the gospel is the story of the saving action promised through the prophets, its purpose is not to warm us beside a cozy fireside but to become the purifying fire of divine love to purge and inflame our hearts. If the gospel is the reality of God's incarnate presence born from Mary's womb, it is not a possession we can safely keep under our control. It is God's power to disrupt, transform, and control our lives, even as it took possession of Mary and Joseph. Handling God's gospel is not like hanging paper chains on a tree. It is like rewiring the Christmas lights while they are plugged in, knowing that at any moment we could be shocked by the electrical power flowing through them.

Second, Paul points to the One who is at the center of our faith: "concerning his Son, who was descended from David according to the flesh and was declared to be Son of God with power according to the spirit of holiness by resurrection from the dead."

The early church did not begin the gospel story in Bethlehem. Mark, the first Gospel, does not even mention Jesus' birth. The earliest proclamation of the good news was centered in the passion, death, and resurrection of Jesus. As time went on, the early Christians worked their way back into the accounts of Jesus' ministry and teaching, back to his birth, and ultimately back to the promises of the prophets. The gospel developed "backwards." The proclamation of the birth of Jesus must be understood from the perspective of his passion, death, and resurrection.

On the basis of human observation Paul knew that Jesus was "descended from David according to the flesh." But it was on the basis of his personal experience of the risen Christ that he came to know Jesus as the "Son of God with power."

The third element at the core of our faith is that this gospel has within it the power to transform our lives. To hear the Christmas story is to be drawn, like Joseph, into the saving action of God. Through Jesus "we have received grace and apostleship to bring about the obedience of faith." To believe this gospel is to enter a new world, to see all of life from a new perspective, and to allow every part of our existence to be transformed by it. The gospel gives us a whole new identity and calling as we respond in obedient faith.

German theologian Jürgen Moltmann wrote that "Jesus is what every human being ought to be— what every human being longs to be—what every human being can be, through faith in him."[8] Many of Charles Wesley's Christmas carols begin at the manger in Bethlehem, but they move on to describe the amazing way in which we can be transformed into the likeness of Christ.

He deigns in flesh to appear,
    Widest extremes to join,
To bring our vileness near,
    And make us all divine;
And we the life of God shall know,
For God is manifest below.

Made perfect first in love,
    And sanctified by grace,
We shall from earth remove,
    And see his glorious face;
His love shall then be fully showed,
And [we] shall all be lost in
    God. [9]

God comes to be one of us, one with us, in the common, natural, ordinary things of life. As we grow in the obedience of our faith, we are transformed into the likeness of the One who is one with us.

How would you describe, in one sentence, your understanding of the central core of the gospel?

What difference does it make for you to read the Christmas story from the perspective of the cross and the Resurrection?

How have you experienced your life being transformed into the likeness of Christ?

[1]From *The Seven Storey Mountain*; page 178.

[2] From *Christian Year and Occasional Hymns*; page 13.

[3] From *The Seven Storey Mountain*; page 178.

[4] From *The Seven Storey Mountain*; page 184.

[5] From *Christian Year and Occasional Hymns*; page 13.

[6] From *The Seven Storey Mountain*; pages 210-11.

[7] From *Christian Year and Occasional Hymns*; page 13.

[8] From *The Way of Jesus Christ,* by Jürgen Moltmann (SCM Press Ltd, 1990); page 60.

[9] From *Christian Year and Occasional Hymns*; page 15.

"Being's Source Begins to Be"

Scriptures for Christmas Day:
Isaiah 52:7-10
Hebrews 1:1-4
John 1:1-14

Near the conclusion of the C. S. Lewis classic *The Chronicles of Narnia,* the children share this conversation that I have often thought would make a wonderful Christmas card.

"It seems, then," said Tirian, smiling himself, "that the Stable seen from within and the Stable seen from without are two different places."

"Yes," said the Lord Digory. "Its inside is bigger than its outside."

"Yes," said Queen Lucy. "In our world too, a Stable once had something inside it that was bigger than our whole world."[1]

Speaking more directly, Lewis said that if what the gospel says happened at Christmas is true, it is "the central event of the history of the Earth."[2]

The lessons for Christmas Day proclaim the cosmic significance of the Incarnation. Something happened in the Bethlehem stable that is bigger than anything else in human history. These lessons open our eyes to *see* the living Word, born out of creation's creation, shaped by the Divine imagination out of which all things came into existence. In Bethlehem's stable, the Source of all life became human life.

The prophetic word from Isaiah introduces a messenger who brings the good news: "Your God reigns." God has acted to fulfill the hope of salvation. The writer of the Epistle to the Hebrews announces that the Word of God, which the prophets had made known in partial and fragmentary ways, has now been made known in the Son. The life born among us in Bethlehem is the life out of which creation came, the One who bears "the exact imprint of God's very being." The opening words of the Fourth Gospel stretch our imagination to see the eternal Word by which everything came into being as the Word that became flesh in Jesus.

Heard together, they create a theological *tour de force* bigger than anything else in our world.

A great risk for many of us is that we will become so familiar with the nativity story, so comfortable with our Christmas traditions, and so cozy in our candlelight celebrations that we miss the shocking magnitude of the gospel we proclaim. Charles Wesley never lost his sense of astonishment at the good news of God's salvation. We can feel his sense of surprise in the exclamation marks and italics he used in the original publication of this carol.

Glory be to God on high,
  And peace on earth descend;
God comes down; he bows the sky,
  And shows himself our friend!
God, the invisible *appears*,
  God, the blest, the great I AM,
Sojourns in this vale of tears,
  And Jesus is his name.
. . . .
Emptied of his majesty,
  Of his dazzling glories shorn,
Being's source *begins* to be,
  And God himself is born![3]

These lectionary texts surprise, shock, and overwhelm us with the amazing word we celebrate at Christmas. They inspire us to respond as Wesley did:

Knees and hearts to him we bow,
  Of our flesh and of our bone,
Jesus is our brother now,
  And God is all our own![4]

"YOUR GOD REIGNS!"
Isaiah 52:7-10

During my first visit to Windsor Castle, the tour guide pointed out that the queen's standard was flying on the mast above the round tower. The flag indicated that members of the royal family were in residence. We toured the public areas of the castle with an absurd expectation that at any moment we might bump into Elizabeth, Phillip, or one of the children. It never happened, of course; but the flag on the mast was the sign that the Windsors were in charge.

The flying of the royal standard became a powerful symbol in the aftermath of the death of Princess Diana. In previous times of crisis the tradition of not lowering the flag over Buckingham Palace signified stability. In this case, it became a symbol of the British struggle with the role of the monarchy. Finally, in a huge accommodation to public pressure, the flag was lowered to half staff; but it still flew as the symbol of the queen's presence and authority.

In Isaiah's day the Hebrew people faced a gigantic theological crisis. Their faith was rooted in the conviction that the Almighty God had taken up residence in the Temple in Jerusalem and that God's faithfulness was tied to the stability of David's monarchy. The fall of Jerusalem in 587 B.C. brought an end to the monarchy, the destruction of the Temple, and the exile of the people. Their world had fallen apart; their faith was unhinged from its center. The symbol of their stability was gone; they were forced to rethink everything they believed, hoped, and trusted.

Isaiah brought a word of comfort and hope to the people in exile. Chapter 52 opens with a wake-up call to the people of Zion that sounds like an invitation to a party. "Awake, awake . . . . Put on your beautiful garments . . . . Shake yourself from the dust, rise up" (verses 1:1-2). In the lectionary reading, Isaiah paints the picture of a royal messenger, running across the mountains that separated the people from their homeland. He comes with the announcement: "Your God reigns." The royal standard flies on the mast again. The Lord has taken up residence among the people.

The words of the prophet capture the spirit of the good news that we celebrate in the birth of Jesus. Let's face it: sometimes we all feel as if this world is out of control. No flag flies on the royal mast; no one seems to be in charge. We feel likc people in exile: alone, isolated, without hope or stability in a chaotic, violent, and oppressive world. There seems to be little reason to rejoice when we are confronted with the pain, injustice, and suffering around us. But then we see, faintly at first, but progressively more clearly, a messenger who comes with good news: Christ has been born. God has not given up on this world. Your hope for peace is not in vain. In this child we can *see* the salvation of God

already present with us that will one day be fulfilled. His flag has been raised on this confused and broken world. Your God reigns. Rejoice!

Our worship team has an annual discussion about how to conclude the Christmas Eve candlelight service. Should we send the worshipers out in the gentle, awe-filled glow of "Silent Night"? Or should we conclude with the explosion of "Joy to the World"? There's never any question in my mind; I am on the side of joy. Having heard the gospel story and having received the light of Christ, we are sent into a dark world as messengers of the good news of God's reign among us in Jesus. Like the musical notes descending the scale in the opening lines of the hymn, God descended into our world and raised the banner of saving love over all creation.

When have you felt as if you were in exile? Does this world seem "out of control" to you? What experiences of life have shattered your faith?

How have you seen or experienced the hope that the prophet offered to the exiles?

Read the words of the song "Joy to the World" carefully. What difference does it make in your life to believe that "the Lord is come"?

GOD THE INVISIBLE APPEARS
Hebrews 1:1-4

Communication can be tough, even at Christmas. A United

Methodist bishop remembers that his family was driving to the church on Christmas Eve when his young son asked, "Dad, are you going to let us enjoy Christmas this year, or are you going to try to explain it?" The good news we proclaim at Christmas goes beyond our human explanation, precisely because it is good news about the action of God.

A friend who was surfing the Internet typed in the word *GOD*. He was amazed at what he found. Alta Vista located 1,784,736 web sites for God and told him he needed to categorize his search. This response proves that when you start searching for God, you need to have some idea of who you are looking for. Another search engine said, "There was no response. The server could be done or is not reporting." I suspect that may be how a lot of folks feel when they pray. His favorite was a God website that announced:

This God Website is to prove to the rational skeptic the existence of God, and then to lead him to God, once the idea of God is appropriated.

The God of the Bible is not a cosmic computer in the sky. This is the passionate, loving God who connects with people in the deepest part of their being. This is the God who takes the initiative and seeks to communicate infinite love to us.

The writer of Hebrews says that God tried "in many and various ways" to get the word to us through the prophets. Paul said that God attempted to communicate through the created order (Romans 1:19-20). But the message never quite got through, at least not to God's satisfaction. The result was that "in these last days [God] has spoken to us by a Son." Having attempted every other means of communication, God sent a baby.

Nothing is more common to human existence than the fact that every human being is born from a woman's womb. There is no other way to get into this world. All humanity shares this experience.

That is just the point. God comes to us in this very real, very fragile, very vulnerable moment of existence. This is the God who meets us in human flesh, with all its strength and weakness, all its joy, and all its pain. The astonishing good news of the Incarnation is that the Almighty God meets us in the moment when we are utterly human. God comes to us, not when we are the most religious, but when we are the most real. God comes, not when we attempt to be humanly perfect, but when we are perfectly human. God comes, not when we work at being strong, but when we acknowledge that we are weak. God comes, not when we stare off into some ethereal space in search of an angel, but when we find a baby in Bethlehem, born into human flesh just like every one of us.

The God who spoke indirectly

through the prophets has now spoken directly through a Son. Just as a human child bears the inescapable marks of human parents ("You have your father's eyes! You have your mother's toes!"), this Son "is the reflection of God's glory and the exact imprint of God's very being." Eugene Peterson's paraphrase reads, "The Son perfectly mirrors God, and is stamped with God's nature."[5]

Some folks ask, "How much of God was there in Jesus?" I suspect the best answer is, "All that God could cram into a human body." The claim of the epistle is not that "all" of God was packaged up in Jesus but that "all" of Jesus mirrored the essential character and being of God. If you want to know what God is like, just look at the Son.

The writer fills these verses with huge affirmations. The Son, he declares, created all things and sustains all things by his power. He is the divinely chosen heir of all things. In his sacrificial love he "made purification" for our sins and is now seated "at the right hand of the Majesty on high." Taken together, the affirmations lift before us a composite image of the cosmic significance of the cross and the resurrection of Jesus Christ, which also speaks to the deepest needs of our souls.

I know the woman who received the best Christmas gift in Tampa last year. In August she had been diagnosed with severe cardiomyopathy, a rare heart disorder that causes the muscle of the heart to become inflexible. The condition is generally terminal. The only medical cure is a heart transplant.

Week by week the woman became progressively weaker as she waited for a donated heart. At 2:00 A.M. on a dark, cold night just before Christmas, she was awakened with the news that a heart was on the way. By 4:00 A.M., the heart was in her chest. By 10:00 A.M., she was out of surgery and on her way to recovery. When I talked with her about her new heart, she said, "You know, this was the second time that someone died for me." Her Christmas gift came from some unknown person who died and gave her a new heart. But she knew that long ago Jesus, the Son of God, had died and risen again so that she might inherit the gift of new life.

In what essential ways are you like your parents?

What does it mean for you to say that "God spoke through a Son"?

How does this affirmation about Jesus influence the way we understand the Bible?

"WHAT IF GOD WERE ONE OF US?"
John 1:1-14

———

How many times across the weeks of Advent have you heard someone say, "Ah, now that's what Christmas is all about!"?

Children with stars in their eyes

gaze in amazement at the lights of a Christmas tree; and the world says, "That's what Christmas is all about."

A Norman Rockwell painting pictures a family gathered around a perfectly laden dinner table where a perfectly browned turkey waits for the father's carving knife. This perfect three-generation, nuclear family pauses for prayer; and the world says, "Now, that's what Christmas is all about."

Skaters glide in perfect precision beneath a gigantic tree in Rockefeller Center while the Rockettes kick up their heels at Radio City Music Hall; and the world says, "That's what Christmas is all about."

Church volunteers ring bells for the Salvation Army, collect toys for children, serve meals at a homeless shelter; and the world says, "That's what Christmas is all about."

These, and a million memories like them, are beautiful gifts of the Christmas season; but the writer of the Fourth Gospel declares, "That's NOT what Christmas is all about!" The good news we celebrate is not about anything that we do; it is about what God has done. Christmas is about the shocking intrusion of God into human history in ways that totally transform our existence. It is about the amazing way in which the God who created all things comes to be one of us. It is about the Light that shines among us, even when we continue to walk in darkness. It is about the way God gives power for every one of us to become a child of God. It is about the Word that became flesh and dwelt among us, full of grace and truth.

Make no mistake about it: if what we announce at Christmas actually happened, it is the biggest thing that ever happened on the planet earth. God—the infinite, all-powerful creator—became one of us.

In a classic expression of cross-generational miscommunication, we were gathered around the Christmas dinner table when my daughter told her grandmother that she had given her boyfriend a CD for Christmas. Her grandmother was impressed, overly impressed, actually. We spent the next hour explaining to one generation that a CD was something you play and explaining to the other generation that a CD was something you save. In the process of the conversation, we talked about a rock song by Joan Osborn that was making its way across the pop charts that year. The singer wondered if God had a name what it would be. Or if God had a face, what would it look like? The recurring question in the refrain was, "What if God were one of us?"

The writer of John's Gospel is the philosopher of the four Gospel writers. This Gospel never reports the familiar details of the Nativity story. There are no shepherds, no angels, no baby born in a stable. John does not tell us what happened but tells us what it means. And to do that, he goes all the way

MEET THE SON OF GOD

back before the beginning of time.

"In the beginning. . ." Suddenly, our ears perk up. We have heard that before. They are the first words of the first sentence in the first chapter of the first book in the Bible: "In the beginning when God created the heavens and the earth." And how did God do all that creating? In Genesis, God *speaks* creation into being. John does not stop with the spoken word of God. He takes us behind the creating Word to the Word that was the thought, the idea, in the divine imagination of God.

I saw a box of Lincoln Logs in the mall and immediately remembered the year my brother and I got Lincoln Logs for Christmas. I recalled how we pictured in our imaginations all the things we would build, and I was reminded that everything that comes into being begins with a thought, an idea in the imagination of the creator.

The Gospel begins with the Word, the thought or idea in the creative imagination of God. The Word was so much a part of God's existence that it was a part of God's very being. That creative Word, John says, "became flesh and lived among us."

We need to hear those words in all their naked, offensive power. The Divine Word, the perfect expression of God's creative intention for creation, settled down into the womb of Mary. Then that Child developed just the way each of us grew in the womb. And when gestation was complete, that Child was born in water, blood, sweat, and tears, just the way every one of us is born into this world. And he grew among us, fully human, just like every one of us.

With wonderful simplicity, E. Stanley Jones wrote: "Jesus is God simplified. God approachable, God understandable, God lovable . . . Jesus puts a face on God."[6]

What difference does the Word made flesh make in your life and mine? John describes two potential responses. "He came to what was his own, and his own people did not accept him." Some rejected Jesus, and some still do. "But to all who received him, who believed in his name, he gave power to become children of God." To all who with stumbling and inadequate faith dare to believe that in Jesus, God has been present with us, God gives power—the same creative power that spoke forth creation—to become something we could never become on our own: the children of God.

Here is the point: the Son of God became a child to enable all of us to become children of God. The Word became flesh among us in Jesus so that the Living Word might become flesh within every one of us. The momentous alternative of the gospel is that God becomes one of us so that every one of us might become one with God!

See there; the new-born Saviour see,

By faith discern the great I AM;

'Tis he! the Eternal God; 'tis he
That bears the mild Immanuel's name.

The Prince of peace on earth is found,
The Child is born, the Son is given,
Tell it to all the nations round,
Jehovah is come down from heaven.
Jehovah is come down to raise
His dying creatures from their fall,
And all may now receive the grace
Which brings eternal life to all.

Lord, *we* receive thy grace, and thee
With joy unspeakable receive,
And rise thine open face to see,
And one with God for ever live.[7]

Charles Wesley

How does it change your understanding of the meaning of Christmas to see it from the perspective of John 1:1-14?

If God became a child so that all of us can become children of God, what changes need to be made in your life to fulfill God's saving purpose for you?

Where have you met the Son of God during this study?

---

[1] From *The Last Battle,* by C. S. Lewis (Macmillan, 1970); pages 140-41.

[2] From *Miracles,* by C. S. Lewis (Touchstone Books, 1996); page 108.

[3] From *Wesley Hymns;* no. 143.

[4] From *Christian Year and Occasional Hymns;* page 45.

[5] From *The Message;* page 539.

[6] From *The Word Became Flesh,* by E. Stanley Jones (Abingdon Press, 1963); pages 37, 48.

[7] From *Christian Year and Occasional Hymns;* page 45.